DEAR CULTURE

DEAR CULTURE

MONIQUE O'NEAL

RBH Professional Development Institute, LLC

Copyright © 2021 by Monique O'Neal

All rights reserved.
No part of this publication may be reproduced, distributed or transmitted in any form or by any means, without prior written permission.

Published by:
RBH Professional Publishing, a division
RBH Professional Development Institute
2000 Town Center, Suite 1900
Southfield, MI 48075
www.rbhprofessionalpublishing.com

Book Design by:

Library of Congress Control Number: 2021902062

ISBN 978-1-7339533-6-8
eISBN 978-1-7339533-7-5

Printed in the United States of America

Dedication

"To my granny whose silent smiles and quiet laughter
taught me how to be her wildest dreams"
In Loving Memory
Sarah E. O'Neal "Tee Tee"
1920-2014

The Brown Crayon (Prelude)

There are various colors in a box of crayons. They are all used for different things in different ways. In this box is a crayon that doesn't get used as much as all the other crayons. Sometimes it gets used to shade in small spots or give things a more natural look. It isn't as beautiful as a light green or a rose pink or a cream orange. The brown crayon might almost never get used in an important masterpiece but it is still an option among all of these other colors. The brown crayon may sit while all the other colors are being used and sharpened and reused again. The protective paper may have to be torn off these colors for better use. Some have been broken in half or even thrown away. Still the brown crayon is staying strong and waiting for its time to be used. Soon less and less crayons make their way to the box. Making the box feel so empty. The brown crayon will soon start to stand out because of its fresh look and neat cover. See all these other crayons were feeling so important and empowered because they were being used every time. Not knowing that soon their time would come to an end. They had the power to make a masterpiece stand out. See the brown crayon knew what it felt like to have power, not being used was its blessing. Because now that we are down to the last of the crayons in the box it's finally getting the attention it has patiently waited for. It might not be to give the most vibrant of colors but it gives the most natural, beautiful shade of color could ever give. The brown crayon may now shine and can encourage any crayon to wait their turn. Stay humble, stay motivated, and stay focused. Your turn is coming. Don't let the sight of power deter you from your true potential.

.

These poems are for those who need some self-encouragement. Change the "You Are" to "I am" and let the manifestation of positive words bring you peace.

Contents

Dedication		v
The Brown Crayon (Prelude)		vii
1	Hi from Me	1
2	A Dedication	4
3	Raise the Flag for the Culture	7
4	Dear White Privilege	10
5	Dear Black Brother	13
6	Blue Lights	16
7	His Last Moments	19
8	The After Talk	23
9	Abandoned	26
10	It Feels Like We Can't	29
11	Dear Son	32
12	Black Encouragement	35
13	We Stand	38

14	Dear Beautiful Black Women	41
15	Better Than Yesterday	44
16	Dear Single Mother	47
17	Continue to Fight	49
18	We are DONE	52
19	Unapologetically Black	54
20	The Marathon Continues	56

About The Author   58

I

Hi from Me

I am not your average black girl

I got a different mindset of how I see this crazy world

While people are beefing and tearing each other down

I am smiling and laughing trying to hold my own self down

I am watching my own back and keeping my head above the clouds

I run in small groups because I get nervous in crowds

If I hear someone speaking negative over my name

I ignore it because I know that going back and forth is so lame

I don't look to other people to fulfill my needs and dreams

I keep it moving plotting on my own master plan, I don't need a team

See this world is full of robbers and snakes

Sometimes I can't tell who is real or fake

It's sad when I have to look over my shoulder every day

Always keeping one eye open every night no matter where I lay

I pray to God that this world will change into something greater

We just have to join hands and speak out together

Learn to be stronger and ignore the negativity

Try spreading love, peace, and positivity

Remember to stand strong being the change we want to see

Because I know this change will have to start with me

YOU

ARE

LOVED

2

A Dedication

This is dedicated to the father with two jobs trying to keep a happy home

Just know God is going to be whether hot or cold

This is dedicated to the single mother trying to keep a roof over her kid's head

Just know that you can do anything because God rose from the dead

This is dedicated to the teenage girl being peer pressured into having sex

Just know that your body is temple and nothing less

This is dedicated to the teenage boy being pushed into selling drugs

Just know God has a path for you than being a thug

This is dedicated to the druggies and alcoholics trying to get clean

Just know God hears your prayers and sees every dream

This is dedicated to the homeless who are trying to do everything to get off the street

Just know God can do anything all you have to do is believe

This dedicated to all those out there that have no hope in their life

Just know God is going to be there every day and night

YOU

ARE

BRAVE

3

Raise the Flag for the Culture

I promise to always love being black

No matter the skill or knowledge that people may say I lack

I promise to remain smart and strong

Even when the system fails me and does me wrong

I promise to love my people and lift them up

Because the world is turning against us and becoming corrupt

I promise to build myself my own brand

And to not worry about who is and isn't my number one fan

I promise to let God do his work and wait on his plan

Because they want us to kill each other and put each other in the ground

I promise to not let people talk me down or make me feel less than what I know I am worth

Because I've been somebody since birth

I promise to be proud of the heritage that I originated from and to celebrate it everyday

No matter the looks I might get and the negative comments that people might say

I am BLACK and I am PROUD

I promise to say it whether alone or in a crowd!

YOU

ARE

GIFTED

4

Dear White Privilege

Dear white privilege, you have been permanently denied!

We will no longer be accepting your ignorance! We are officially tired

No more looking down on us and making us feel small

Because the taller you are the harder you fall

We are no longer accepting your smart remarks or dirty looks

Because guess what you aren't the only ones who can read books

No more making us feel like we aren't educated or more qualified

Because we will never give up and if we fail at least we tried

We are no longer accepting your disloyal leadership or rules

Because you really think we are a bunch of fools

No more letting you all win at every race

Because when this is all over we will have a trophy in our case

YOU

ARE

APPROACHABLE

5

Dear Black Brother

Dear Black Brother, I see you trying to be better

Keep your head up it won't always be stormy weather

The storm will soon pass and people will see your true potential

That your skills are not useless but they are essential

One day you'll rise to the top and be the boss and "the man"

Those people who put you down will soon try and be your number one fan

Please ignore the hate and the grimy criticism that people throw at you

Because God wouldn't give you anything too hard he didn't think you couldn't get through

So rise above the negative comments and the ugly looks

Because they hate and are scared of an educated black man who knows what he is talking about

They expect you to complain and throw fits and pout

They don't want you to grow to become successful and earn a high rank

They want you to be like ship with holes in the bottom and just sank

But I am here to tell you, you are STRONG, SMART, and SOPHISTICATED to the highest degree

Just look in the mirror and you will see what I see

YOU

ARE

CONFIDENT

6

Blue Lights

When you see those blue and white flashes behind you, you ever feel beads of sweat pop up on your head

Visions of a black man lying in the street dead

A mother crying and screaming as she looks at her son face down

A crowd of people around her whispering but also not trying to make a sound

Ambulance lights flashing and a man roping off the area with yellow tape

Police officers trying to find out what happened because one of their own careers is at stake

Sadness turns into anger and revenge

A riot of protestors set out to avenge

To stand up for the death of our own who did nothing but buy a snack

We are mad at the cultural knowledge you lack

We are mad at the way you abuse this so called power you so call have

The way you look at us and laugh

Because you see the pain of a hurting race

We are giving you so much grace

We could tear down those walls of racial and distasteful remarks you have for us

But we are humble and meek, we will wait for our time

Just know one day we are going to rise up and shine

One day we are going to be the people that are behind you

We are going to be the people in blue

YOU

ARE

STRONG

7

His Last Moments

1, 2, 3 Clear

The words echoed in my ear

Where was the air for me to breathe?

Why could I not feel my heart beat?

1, 2, 3 Clear

I hear again in my bloody ear

Is that a bullet hole?

I can feel that pain in my soul

1, 2, 3 Clear

I hear these words again in my ear

Opening my eyes I saw a bright light

Feeling like my body was taking flight

1, 2, 3 Clear

These words I could barely hear

A lady screaming in the crowd

It was so desperate and so loud

1, 2, 3 Clear

These words not ringing in my ear

The voices fade

And on the sidewalk I laid

1, 2, 3 Clear

Try one more time please "I'm here"

Pick me up and check my pulse please

Don't leave my body on the scene

1, 2, 3 Clear

My soul cries out with hot salty tears

I didn't even have a gun

I didn't even try and run

1, 2, 3 Clear

I guess I am no longer someone to fear

I am finally going to my peaceful home

I am sorry I had to leave but I will never be GONE

YOU

ARE

FEARLESS

8

The After Talk

What did you see?

I saw you kill me

You reached behind your back I knew you had a gun

I bet you also thought I was gone run

I wanted you to keep your hands in the air

No you really wanted me dead right then and there

I wanted you to comply with the words I was telling you

So why did you shoot?

I was scared you would kill me first

I was trying to record

Why record something when I just wanted some respect

Because it was the tone of your dialect

You weren't listening to anything I said

Well it doesn't matter now because I am dead

So what do I tell them?

You say that you killed him..

YOU

ARE

APPROACHABLE

9

Abandoned

They put hand cuffs on us without even knowing our name

The color of our skin is enough for them to lock us up in chains

We get treated even worse if we open our mouths

They come and snatch people out of their houses

Kids left without a mother or father; looking at them through glass while they talk on the phone

They hold on to that pain of their parents being taken away until they are grown

Don't trust the police is all they know to believe

Having their parents taken away so early taught them nothing but how to grieve

Shedding a tear for someone they will never really get to know

Trying to make it in this world barely knowing where to go

Looking for love in all the wrong places

Trying to find who they are in all the wrong faces

They will never understand what it feels like to lose someone who isn't even dead

YOU

ARE

BLESSED

10

It Feels Like We Can't

We can't live here!

If we have to live in fear

We can't do anything right

All we can do is protest and fight

You are making us look like we are such bad people

But this is a land where we are supposed to be treated equal

We can't sleep here!

Because we sleep in fear

We wake up hoping to come home at night

But some of us don't, and that's not right

The people that are supposed to protect us are killing us

Or putting us on a bus

Either way we probably won't ever see the light of day

Especially if they have anything to say

We don't belong here!

That has been very clear.

We are trying to live in peace

But your violence has to seize

We are going to have to come to a common ground

No more killing the black or brown

YOU

ARE

POWERFUL

11

Dear Son

Dear Son, Remember that I love you more than life itself

Nothing can tear us apart, not even death

You will always live forever in my heart

I have loved you unconditionally from the start

From the time I heard your little heart beat

Until the first time I heard the pitter patter of your little feet

You have been my little prince and my soldier

I just want you to be the best man you can be when you grow older

Remember that respect is not given it is earned

Patience is a virtue so always remember to wait your turn

Don't rush your blessings because they can turn into a curse

And I rather be holding you in my arms than riding behind you in a hearse

You have a mind of your own and future that is bright

Let God lead you, let him be your light

I want you to live out your dreams and become a great man

I will always be your number one fan

So son stay my baby and never grow up on me

You'll always be my love, baby boy you hold the key

YOU

ARE

INTELLIGENT

12

Black Encouragement

Keep your head up, a smile on your face, and hope in your heart

Pray to God that you and Him will never get far apart

Love your family, friends, and associates

When you feel like giving up, just wait because God isn't done with you yet

Encourage yourself to be a better you everyday

Block out negativity that people that don't know you might say

But those are the things that build your character

This is your story and you're the author

No matter where you go GOD will be right there

Just know God would never give you more than you can bear

He has His arms wrapped around you and looks down on you from the heavens above

He will always surround you with peace and love

Even if where you lay is even for a day

Remember to pray before you lay

YOU

ARE

AMAZING

13

We Stand

We stand in this black line representing for the ones who paved the way

We stand up with our fist thrown up in the sky to represent that we have something to say

We stand up locked arm in arm to show our unity

We stand up with each other because we are a community

We stand up for rights

We stand up not to be rebellious or to get into fights

We stand up for those who couldn't

We stand up for those who were told they shouldn't

We stand up because we can!

We stand up because we have trust in a God who always has a greater plan

YOU

ARE

HARDWORKING

14

Dear Beautiful Black Women

Your melanin skin is the first thing people are going to see

Not recognizing your potential or college degree

They don't care about your bright smile or confidence

They will not give you sympathy for all the struggles you have to balance

All they want to see is the "angry black women" for their own entertainment

Or watch you cry over your dead son on the pavement

They want you to struggle to raise your young boys into men

They want them to drop out of school and either be in the streets or locked up in the pen

Raise your daughters to be as strong and as great as you are

Encouraging them that they don't have to show skin to go far

But use that as encouragement to raise your girls and boys as kings and queens

Soon they will know you love them every day and that you got their backs

And that you will always pick up where they may slack

Tell them to not be afraid to immerse themselves in the things they love

Because they will always have help from the Man above

YOU

ARE

SUCCESSFUL

15

Better Than Yesterday

Wake up with a smile on your face and love in your heart

Open your eyes to the light and forget about the dark

Walk with the strength that God is right behind you

And pray with faith before anything you do

Love unconditionally with all your soul

You know the world is not a nice place, so don't let it turn you cold

Believe in yourself more than anyone else could

But also love yourself more than anyone else would

Know your worth that is key to having the power

Make every day a beautiful springtime and bloom into a flower

Be more than you can imagine and have nothing but faith

Because today is the day to begin your race

YOU

ARE

FREE

16

Dear Single Mother

This is for you who works that nine to five faithfully everyday

This is for you who does the work and never complains about her day

This is for you who provides for her family and sometimes her friends

My grandma used to say a women's work never ends

This is for you making sure all the bills are paid on time

This is for you because even though you always say it, we know you aren't always fine

This is for you because you never gave up even when times were hard

This is for you because you never folded you always held your cards

This is for you because no one ever knows when you are having a hard day

You just got home and close your door and fall to your knees and pray

This is for you raising your beautiful kids without a father

This is for you because you refuse to let down your son or daughter

This is for you because life can get either better or worse at any time

But just know God got you and everything is going to be just fine

17

Continue to Fight

Whatever we do let's not give up or be afraid to fight

Let's throw our fists up and stand up for what is right

We should never be afraid to speak up for our race

Never let anyone make us feel out of place

We deserve respect just as much as anyone else

WE have to make people listen even when they act deaf

WE have to let them know that this world is ours too

And that we will not stop doing what's right, we will not become mute

And if they try to get in our way we won't be timid

Because everybody has their breaking point and this is pushing the limits

We need our men just as much as any other race

So stop trying to push them to a dark place

A place of solitude and no love or respect

Just a place where their mental health becomes a wreck

They just want to tear us down and beat us up

All they want is for our culture to become corrupt

YOU

ARE

MAGICAL

18

We are DONE

We are done being slaves

The streets are now paved

And we will march with our shoes on

Not with feet bare to the bone

We are different and the same

You have our ancestors to blame

Because they walked miles for peace between our races

They had people come from all places

To stand together hand in hand with our sisters and brothers

Rising up out the gutter

To shout out at the top of our lungs "BLACK LIVES MATTER"

We will be over every newsletter

We will take social media by storm and make everyone feel our pain

I told you we are different but the same

Our ancestors bled to show how much they wanted peace

And for that we will continue to preach

We are done being your slaves

We are stronger, smarter and very brave

To stand on these paved streets and tell you "BLACK LIVES MATTER" loud and proud

It's time to take over the world crowd by crowd

19

Unapologetically Black

I will not apologize for my melanin skin or for my kinky, curly hair

I will not apologize for the way my hips sway when I walk or the dramatic tone in my voice when I talk

I will not apologize for laughing with loudness or expressing myself with bold colors on my beautiful brown skin

I will not apologize for my direct opinions or for my way of telling a story with my hands

I will not apologize will not for speaking my mind when I need to or for the way I roll my eyes when I hear something I don't like

I will not apologize for being a strong black woman with an intelligent mind or for always holding my head up high

I will not apologize for wanting to achieve my dreams no

matter how hard it may seem because even Dr. Martin Luther King had a dream

I shall rise to the top with my beautiful, radiant mocha brown skin glistening in the light of success

You will apologize for ever doubting that I could be more than the color of my skin

20

The Marathon Continues

Is this the dream?

The dream of Martin Luther King?

It's more like a nightmare if you ask me

Sometimes I want to blind fold my eyes so I can't see

I don't want to see my brothers and sisters suffering

Is this really the dream?

I am pretty sure this isn't what that dream means

I am pretty sure we aren't holding hands

I don't hear any happy music I am not dancing

I am burying my brothers and sisters

Going to protest rally's to stop the use of pistols

Something that should protect my family, but it's killing them

You ask why they got shot and it was just because somebody saw him

It's time to change our ways

I am still waiting on the better days

You know the ones everyone say they praying for

But have you ever drop to the floor?

Got down on both knees

And told the Lord "Please"

Please Lord protect me as I walk out into this world everyday

Protect my mind and every word I say

So at the end of the day I can come home safe

Because like Martin Luther King I have a dream but first I have to win the race

.... The Marathon Continues , RIP Nipsey Hussle

About The Author

Monique O'Neal is an up and coming millennial author who has created an insightful poetic compilation of fresh socially relevant commentary pieces in her debut literary masterpieces. She is a daughter with NY roots and a southern flavor who has spent the majority of her life below the Mason Dixon lines. From her adoption as a baby and young life spent surrounded by a strong close-knit southern family Monique chose to express herself by putting pen to paper and creating diverse poetic narrations and spoken word

www.ingramcontent.com/pod-product-compliance
Lightning Source LLC
Chambersburg PA
CBHW071320080526
44587CB00018B/3291